𝕹𝖎𝖍𝖎𝖑 𝕺𝖇𝖘𝖙𝖆𝖙:

      STEPHEN T. PRISK, STL

            Censor Librorum

𝕴𝖒𝖕𝖗𝖎𝖒𝖆𝖙𝖚𝖗:

      KEVIN J. SWEENEY, DD

            Bishop of Paterson

Dear Reader,

The gospel is perpetually true, never old, never stale in confronting the world. The world is the gospel's enemy, always and in all places, combating it with different, though simultaneously the same, battles over the course of history.

The alienation, fear, isolation, deprivation and loneliness of being a strange man in a strange land is a theme old as time. Poverty is nothing new. But the mass emigration to the United States from Europe in the late 19th century was very much a new phenomenon. The Church confronted the new challenge of spiritually and physically shepherding her children into a land whose cultural roots as a nation had grown to view the arrival of the Bark of Peter, filled with Catholics, with hostility and disdain.

In such moments of crisis, throughout the two thousand millennial history of the Church, her Divine Founder has always sent the right person at the right time — a person of their age — to help pilot the ship with the map of the gospel, through the tempest that the world threw at it. The map is always applied to successfully sail out the particular storm, and is always accurate despite its age.

And so it was with Frances Xavier Cabrini, a 19th century Italian farm girl with dreams of voyaging East, who was told by her captain that she was needed instead on the ships journey West. There millions of immigrant Catholics suffering from discrimination, bigotry and prejudice. Despite their dreams and aspirations, these new arrivals suffered economic depravity, sickness and marginalization. They also experienced pressures and temptations from the Protestant Americans they encountered to abandon their Catholic faith.

Cabrini arrived with empty pockets and a full heart and immediately began with her sisters to provide for the physical and spiritual needs of God's people in America. They built orphanages, hospitals and schools. They nursed and catechized.

They loved and were loved, but by some they were hated for being Italian and Catholic.

The Cabrini story is a necessary lesson for children. The faith and inspiration of a young farm girl, with the graces of her Heavenly Father, was the launch point of a worldwide missionary order, far beyond the young saint's dreams. Yet, this evangelical apostolate was attacked every step of the way by the enemies of Christ and His Church. This is a valuable lesson for children: the impossible is possible when it is in the name of the Gospel, but the cross will never be lacking on the road to eternal glory.

Patrick A. O'Boyle, Esq.

Our Friend, Mother Cabrini

A children's book from the "Our Friend" series by Amici Santi

A Saint! Have you heard that word before? Do you know what it means? A Saint is somebody who is actually in heaven with God!

God uses people on earth (or who were once on earth) to perform miracles. You can pray for any Saint's intercession (or his/her help) to assist you in your life.

Quite simply, saints are our friends! Let's talk about our friend, St. Frances Xavier Cabrini! She is known by many as Mother Cabrini.

She was born in Italy on July 15, 1850 about two months before expected. Frances was tiny and would remain fragile in health for her whole life.

Philippians 4:13 says, "I can do all things through Christ, who strengthens me."

This was very true for young Frances. With God, she knew she could do great things.

At a young age, she knew she wanted to be a missionary (a person who travels to promote the faith) to China and India. She wanted to evangelize!

Evangelize? What does that mean? She wanted to tell people about God and encourage them to practice the faith.

At a flowing canal by her uncle's house, she would place small violets into paper boats and set them into the water. She would call these flowers her little "missionaries" heading to the East.

When older, she took vows as a religious sister and took on a name after Saint Francis Xavier. She wanted to imitate the great saint who was a missionary in the East. Frances was determined to do the same!

While in Italy, she helped care for orphans, taught children, and more.

Her good work welcomed the attention of the Pope! This was her opportunity to pursue her dream: to go East!

"The Lord is my shepherd; I shall not want." - Book of Psalms

As we learn sometimes, God's plans are different from our plans. Pope Leo XIII needed somebody to help her countrymen and women who were moving to the United States.

His orders were clear: "Not to the East, but to the West." Frances wanted to go to the East her entire life. The Holy Spirit had other plans for her: to help the Italians in America.

At first, Archbishop of New York didn't think this tiny nun (who barely spoke English) would be able to help.

He advised her to return to Italy.

But she had her orders from the Pope. With hard work and prayers, she knew God would lead their mission.

In time, she helped the Italians stay close to God. How did she do this? She founded religious classes, schools, orphanages, and hospitals.

She had no money or resources. But she would tell her sisters, "With five pennies and God, I can accomplish many great things."

These victories were miracles! And there were many more to come.

One time, she wanted to establish a larger orphanage for the children in her care. She agreed to buy land that had no well water.

Frances was not worried. She prayed for the Blessed Virgin Mary's intercession. In a dream, Mary told Frances where to dig for water.

The next day, Frances told her team where to dig and... out popped a mountain spring. A miracle!

In time, her hard work was requested around the United States. Miracles kept occurring!

Another time, Frances and the nuns were searching for an orphanage location. During their walk, a lady offered the nuns a ride back to the convent.

Frances told the lady a dream she had with a very specific vision of this property to home the orphanage.

The lady was in shock since she owned the property that Frances was describing. She offered the property to Frances and the orphans. A miracle!

The Pope was so happy that Frances brought so many of her countrymen and women back to the church.

When he asked her what she planned to do next, She insisted on helping others in places such as Brazil and Argentina. He joked that she didn't speak Portuguese, or Spanish. She smiled as she reminded him that she barely spoke English when she first arrived in the United States.

He blessed her next mission and she was on her way.

After Mother Cabrini died, another famous miracle occurred. In a New York City hospital, a baby boy was accidentally treated with the wrong eye medication. The mistake would normally cause the baby to lose his eyesight.

The Nuns prayed for Mother Cabrini's intercession all night long. When inspecting the baby the next morning, the doctor was expecting the baby to be blind.

But instead, the doctor was looking at two perfect eyes! A miracle!

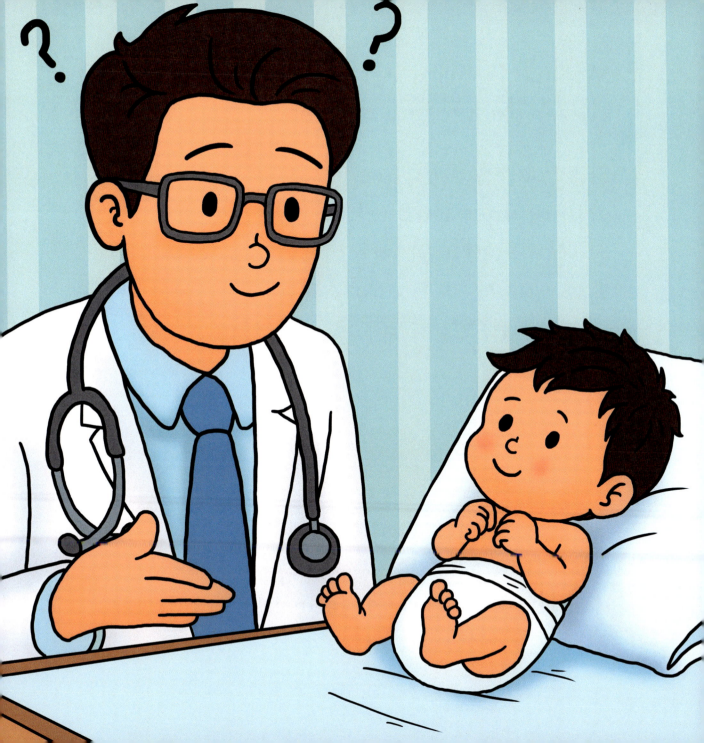

Mother Cabrini is the first American citizen to become a saint!

She founded 67 hospitals, schools, and orphanages throughout the United States, South America, Europe and more. God wants us to imitate the saints' lives. Like what, start a school? Well, some may.

But mostly, we must imitate their courage.

Mother Cabrini's goal was not to start hospitals, schools, and orphanages. She did these things to achieve her mission: to get people into Heaven!

People all around the world still pray for Mother Cabrini's help.

And you need to know something very important. You can pray for her help!

All the saints, like Mother Cabrini, are our friends. If you need something very big, or very small, you can always ask for their help. And don't forget, they want to help you!

A Mother Cabrini prayer

I VENERATE and greet thee, O most blessed Mother Cabrini in the sweetest Heart of Jesus Christ, and I congratulate thee with all my heart on that honour wherewith thou wast honoured by God and by all the court of Heaven on this the day of thine entrance therein. And for the increase of thy joy and thy glory I offer thee that same transcendently precious and worthy Heart of Jesus Christ, beseeching thee that thou wouldst deign to pray to God for me, and to assist me in the hour of my death. Amen.

Page from another book in the
Amici Santi collection
**Our Friend,
San Gennaro**

What is an intercessory prayer?

"Prayer of intercession consists in asking on behalf of another. It knows no boundaries and extends to one's enemies." - CCC 2647

Saints are our special friends in heaven. A saint cannot answer your prayers directly. But they can take your prayers and lift them up to God and pray for you.

So, if you pray for Mother Cabrini's intercession, you are simply asking for your friend's help! And your friend will lift the prayer up to God!

Will you pray for her help?

Page from another book in the
Amici Santi collection

**Our Nonni, Saints
Joachim and Anne**

Fear and Terror

"I am afraid, I am very afraid, but I trust fully in you. Ah, my sweet Jesus, I tightly embrace your Cross." – Mother Cabrini

The tiny nun was terrified of the ocean. But she would not let fear stop her in her works. She traveled across the ocean 23 times during her life.

Don't forget, it is normal to be afraid. Mother Cabrini leaned on God to help her overcome these fears. No matter what you fear, you can do the same.

Page from another book in the
Amici Santi collection
Our Friend, Saint
Anthony of Padua

Quiz time!

What would Mother Cabrini put into paper boats as a child?

In which country was she born?

What was her fear?

What is a missionary?

When she was little, where did she want to go? East or West?

Page from another book in the
Amici Santi collection

Our Friend, Saint
Anthony the Abbot

Quiz time!

Which group did the pope want Mother Cabrini to help?

How many institutions did she help create?

When a property she purchased had no water, what did she do?

Who was the first American citizen to become a saint?

If she is no longer alive, can I pray for her intercession?

Dear parents, grandparents, + guardians

The "Our Friend" series is dedicated to bringing the colorful lives of the saints directly into children's hands.

These stories can inspire future saints. As Pope Saint Clement I tells us, "Follow the saints because those who follow them will become saints."

God Bless you.

Page from another book in the
Amici Santi collection
La Vigilia,
a Christmas poem

Made in the USA
Monee, IL
22 April 2025

16218716R00029